What My Dog Told Me

About Healthy Eating

or

Animal Communication

Goes Vegan

Mary Ann Cavallaro

©2015 Mary Ann Cavallaro. All rights reserved. Printed in the United States of America. No part of this publication may be reproduced, stored in a retrieval system or transmitted in any form or by any means without the prior written permission of the publisher.

Createspace.com 2015

ISBN-13:9780692524626

Welcome....

If you love dogs but don't see a connection from them to the animals you eat or have been thinking about (or already committed to) a vegetarian or vegan diet that will benefit your health and animals, look no further. If you are curious about animal communication and energy medicine, this book is for you. Author Mary Ann Cavallaro brings over 15 years' experience of following a vegetarian and a vegan life style, practicing the energy moving technique of Therapeutic Touch, and recent experiences with animal telepathy to this book to inform and entertain you.

It offers insight into:

» Motivating examples of animal communication;

» Easy steps to engage in animal communication or Therapeutic Touch;

» And moving from food choices motivated by health to compassion for animals.

Down-to-earth, and filled with personal experience, plus insight from expert animal communicators and animal activists, *What My Dog Told Me About Healthy Eating* makes it easy to understand why one person changed her diet and how you can change yours to be plant rich and animal product poor.

About The Author

Mary Ann Cavallaro is a freelance writer, author and registered nurse. Her articles have appeared in The Princeton Packet, Princeton Magazine, American Vegan and The Nursing Spectrum. The benefit of vegetarian and vegan food choices is a topic of lectures she gives at conferences and hospitals. As an adjunct faculty at Georgian Court University, New Jersey, and St. Francis University, Illinois, she taught Entrepreneurship. MaryAnn lives in Princeton, New Jersey, with her family and communicates daily with her beloved dog, Mochi.

To my brother, Dominic, who motivated me to change my diet;

To my mother, Angela, who encouraged me to "write my stories" and "write a book;"

And to my dog, Mochi,

who opened my eyes to some of the feelings non-human animals.

Table of Contents

1 How I Met My Dog	11
2 Bonding to Mochi Introduces Telepathy	23
3 Display Animals	39
4 Mochi Goes to Syracuse and Uses Her Instincts	47
5 Down on a Grass-Fed Cattle Farm	51
6 My Father, Myself	59
7 Raising Cows and Sending Them to a Slaughter House	67
8 The Look in the Eye	71
9 Talk to Me	77
10 Therapeutic Touch Reaches Animal Communication	83
11 Chip, the Farm Dog	93
12 What She Said	97
Acknowledgments	105
Resources	107

Chapter 1

How I Met My Dog

My name was written on her and her name was written on me.

"That's my dog!" I shouted to my mother, taking my hand off the steering wheel while eagerly pointing at the dog. "That is the kind I want!"

My mother, Angela, and I were driving to Red Bank, New Jersey. Suddenly, I spotted a man walking his dog on the sidewalk, a basset hound. The hound was tri colored, mostly brown with a black coat and white markings. The dog and his person standing under the tree-lined sidewalk made a memorable and charming picture.

My mother, sitting alongside of me in the front seat, said very little. This was unlike her usual conversation style of telling me what to do, or in this case how to drive. Unnoticed by me, my mother was listening intently. She made note of my delight in the hound and related it to a friend of hers who had owned a basset hound. Later she contacted him to find out where he obtained his dog.

During childhood, my family had two dogs, Princey and Queenie. Both were mixed breeds, but when I was a kid, we just called them mutts! Princey was a medium-sized, long haired dog with a curly tail without any major breed identity. Queenie was an unmistakable hound mix. Princey was a feisty male, while Queenie was a mellow female. Although I had more interaction with Princey, who was always getting into trouble, I became hooked on hounds.

I also had shared with a co-worker my wishes to own a basset hound. Returning from a vacation, she had brought me back a tiny detailed glass replica of a basset hound. She had seen it while shopping and had thought of me. The dog replica was tri-colored just like the dog on the sidewalk. I had discussed my breed preferences with my co-worker, but not the colors.

The color match may not have been too coincidental since most bassets have tricolor coats of black, white and tan, or bicolor coats of tan and white. The lighter bicolored coats are called lemons and are a little less common. However, several other unexpected events occurred which I did consider more than coincidence.

I had started my career as a registered nurse, but after several years of practicing nursing in hospitals, I took an opportunity to work in state government as an information technology professional.

My job allowed me to use many of my interests, including writing. When an article I had written for a technical trade journal caught the attention of our IBM representative, I received an invitation to present it at a conference. The conference was being held in Disney World. Excitedly I told a friend about the good news. My friend and her family lived in Dallas, Texas. She surprised me by saying her husband had a business trip to Disney scheduled for the same dates as my trip!

As a rule she did not travel with her husband on work related trips, but since their daughter was experiencing some health issues, they decided to do some pampering. My girlfriend planned to bring her daughter on the trip to Disney.

Together we coordinated our flights to Miami. Traveling on different airlines we were able to meet each other at the airport baggage claim area after our planes landed. However, our hotel room reservations, made separately without knowledge of each other's location, were in hotels that stood side by side. We were hotel neighbors! I stayed in the Dolphin Hotel while my girlfriend and family stayed in the Swann Hotel.

After presenting my article, I was free to visit with my friends. We went on exciting water rides, watched colorful medieval shows and all around had a great time at the park. The highlight of the trip was celebrating the daughter's eleventh birthday.

We celebrated at a Chinese restaurant. A huge mural of the China countryside covered the wall next to us. Thinking an eleven year old might need instruction with her chopsticks, I thought I might be of some help. Fortunately before I made the offer, she picked up her chopsticks and began eating like an expert. Although both parents were very concerned about their daughter, the young girl appeared very poised about the present moment as well as her future. It was April 2, 2001.

During those great days in Disney, dogs were the furthest thing from my mind. I was also in a faltering relationship, but even that didn't seem to bother me. I did think of the man I had been seeing several times, and I wondered what the outcome of our relationship would be. As it turned out the relationship ended soon after I returned home. It was actually the break up that spurred me on to finding a pet. I still wanted a dog like the basset hound I had seen on the sidewalk.

In late April, after returning from my trip to Disney, I visited my mother. I was surprised when she told me that she had tracked down the basset and discovered that her friend had bought his dog at a pet shop in Red Bank. This was in the same vicinity where we had seen the man walking his basset not too long ago. Not only had she tracked down the basset but she had already called the pet shop. My mother was not only a determined person, but one who liked dogs.

To purchase a dog from the pet shop my mother found, you "order" one. At that time I had a vague idea that pet shops bought dogs from puppy mills or places that do not treat animals humanely. I knew that obtaining a dog through a breeder was a more humane way to go and obtaining one from a shelter was even better. However, I had tried these routes only to have been told that I was not deemed a suitable owner.

After finding a reputable breeder, I filled out the breeder's application. The application asked for references. I listed a friend and neighbor as the reference. When my reference was contacted by the breeder and it became known that as an adult I had never owned a dog before, I was considered a high risk owner and dropped to the bottom of the breeder's list. My neighbor was saddened about the outcome and I was a little annoyed with the whole situation.

Actually this breeder in question had a basset hound that had a small litter, three puppies. She said she would consider me. However, her first candidate was an older woman whose dog had recently died. The breeder felt this woman needed immediate companionship and I was placed second on the list. Two of the puppies needed to survive in order for me to get a pet. Unhappy that I was knocked down a peg I was still optimistic, but sadly neither of us received a puppy.

According to the breeder, the litter's mother did not produce adequate milk. Her first milk called colostrum somehow lacked needed nutrients. Human breast milk as well as animal breast milk contains antibodies to protect the infant or new born animal. In humans the antibodies are passed to the newborn via placenta in the mother's womb as well as later after birth in breast milk. But in animals there is no passive transfer of antibodies via placenta in the mother's womb. Antibodies need to be actively ingested after birth from the mother's breast milk.

To take it one step further, the newborn animal's stomach is porous for a limited time after birth. This makes the transfer time of antibodies through the porous or open wall of the stomach to the rest of the body crucial.

The breeder tried to save the litter by bottle feeding them the colostrum. I still remember the sadness in her voice when she told me how they all died, one by one.

I then contacted a local basset hound rescue. Numerous conversations with the opinionated manager followed. It was obvious to me by her questions that she would not consider me for receiving a puppy. Since I worked full time and could not spend a lot of time with the dog, I was not a suitable candidate. And again the stigma of never having owned a dog and having no good dog owner track record made me an unsuitable candidate.

So out of the process of elimination or desperation, I turned to the pet shop. On a sunny day in May, I traveled to Red Bank to place my "order". The owner, a young woman, seemed to know her business. She had questions and made recommendations. If I wanted a smaller dog, she suggested a female. She also asked my color preference and I clearly specified that I wanted a "brown" dog. Later I noted she had written down "tri colored." It felt slightly unnatural to be specifying a color. It made me stop and think that prospective pet owners probably request certain colored coats all the time. If prospective owners like me were more flexible, perhaps more dogs would be rescued than "ordered" at pet shops.

Several weeks went by and I called the pet shop to see how things were going. The owner surprised me when she said that she had found a dog for me, but the puppy, which was about nine weeks old, had kennel cough. She told me the dog was being treated by the veterinarian associated with her store. The puppy was not ready to come home with me, but I could visit the dog in her store.

At the first opportunity, I drove down to the store to meet my new friend, all the while wondering if this particular dog would like me. That was my sole criteria for finding the right pet, a dog who would like me. I parked my car on a side street and almost ran into the pet shop. A friendly young blond boy came out of the back area of the store and handed me a thin little puppy! The cute little dog was fidgeting and had a frightened look in her eyes. Feeling her trembling little body, I lifted her up and rested her head and muzzle on my shoulder. She sniffed me and quickly calmed down. I placed her on the floor and when she took a long sniff of my new sneakers, I knew she liked me. Quickly she turned and ran down a store aisle. I shouted in alarm, but the young boy told me not to worry, the puppy was in the store so she could not run away.

I named her Mochi. The young boy at the pet shop seemed to like the name, unlike many of my friends. Why the name of Mochi? What does Mochi mean? These were the questions my friends asked. One friend went so far as to tell me that I should give the dog a "proper name." I suppose that would mean Snoopy, Lady, or maybe Cleo, a popular basset hound of the 1950s TV show "People's Choice."

My co-worker, who had presented me with the tiny basset replica, suggested the name of "Veggie" since, at the time, I was somewhat of a vegetarian. I quickly threw out that idea.

Several years before I met Mochi, due to health reasons, I had changed my diet. I started by avoiding red meat and dairy. This was not a difficult change and was not made in consideration of the treatment of animals. My health was my sole motivator.

Two years later when my health issues became more critical, I adopted a macrobiotic diet. This diet excludes meat and dairy with focus on how the food is cooked. Macrobiotics however does not exclude fish. The way I like to describe a person who follows a macrobiotic diet is, "A vegan who eats fish." As you may know, a vegan does not eat any animal products. Excluding meat and dairy from my diet was not a problem. However a macrobiotic diet also eliminates the use of sugar. This was a problem.

The first dessert or sweet food that I found included on the diet was a rice cake called Mochi. You can buy it in most health food stores and some supermarkets. Mochi was always a treat, something special. It seemed a great fit, a perfect name for a special dog.

A couple of weeks later, I went back to the store to take Mochi home with me. What I saw made me unhappy. Her eyes were very glassy.

"She may have ear mites," the owner explained with a sound of callousness in her voice. "We put ear cleanser in her ears, which may be causing her eyes to be glassy."

Another reminder of where she came from - the puppy mill.

The color of her fur also caused me some concern. It looked very healthy, but she had a lot of black in her coat. I had specifically asked for a "brown" dog. The owner assured me that she was the classic tri color and would become browner as time went on. I remained skeptical.

With a pleased look on her face, the owner related her story of how she obtained Mochi. A middle person buys the puppy from the puppy mill and brings the animal to the store. The owner said she turned away the first dog brought to her, because "it did not have the look of a basset hound." I have always doubted her story, but I do think back and wonder what happened to that puppy if it existed.

The owner reminded me that Mochi previously had kennel cough and she might cough up some mucous. But since she had been treated with antibiotics, she should be fine. Only if she coughed up copious amounts of mucous, which was highly unlikely, should I take action.

The owner and I sat down and reviewed Mochi's papers. I wrote out a check for $850.00 before New Jersey state tax and paid the bill. I put Mochi in a small borrowed travel case and took her home naively never suspecting that life was going to change.

It was not until several weeks later, while at home reviewing Mochi's papers again, that I saw Mochi was born on April 2, 2001, the day after April Fool's Day and the date of the birthday celebration in Disney World.

Perhaps when I let go of focusing on me and focused on the wellbeing of another, like my friend's daughter, good things are retuned. For me Mochi was that gift.

What My Dog Told Me About Healthy Eating

Chapter 2

Bonding to Mochi Introduces Telepathy

> *"When he just sits loving and knows that he is being loved, those are the moments that I think are precious to a dog; when, with his adoring soul coming through his eyes, he feels that you are really thinking of him."*
>
> John Galsworthy, from *Memories*, 1924

It was at my mother's house that I first saw signs of Mochi's personality.

After religiously watching Barbara Woodhouse videos on puppy training, I was ready for Mochi's arrival with a small green collar and short brown leather leash.

Barbara Woodhouse, an English dog trainer of immense popularly in the United Kingdom in the 1970s and 1980s was the Dog Whisperer, the Cesar Millan of her time. She was to dog training what Julia Child was to cooking.

Woodhouse made countless videos which the Princeton Library owned and I borrowed repeatedly.

Although Woodhouse's career began by training horses, later in life she became best known for her training of dogs. Her book, *No Bad Dogs, The Woodhouse Way,* was a bestseller in 1982. Woodhouse recommended a collar should be on the pet at all times, even in the house. In the event of an emergency, you have something to grab onto. She recommended the short leash to gain better control while walking your dog. For a puppy the size of Mochi, she recommended a cat collar. I bought a green one.

Stopping at my mother's house, I took Mochi out of the travel case wearing her green collar and attached the brown leash.

My mother, with her own dominant personality, immediately wanted to hold Mochi's leash and parade around. My mother took pride in the fact that she grew up in Jersey City, New Jersey, and liked doing things in a flamboyant way. At the time my mother was 85 years old, very fragile and could easily be knocked over. Mochi gently sniffed the hem of her skirt and instinctively did not make any jerky movements. Knowing she was with a fragile person she did not jump up on my mother. With Mochi, my mother was always perfectly safe.

Bonding to Mochi Introduces Telepathy

Mochi also expressed her feelings about being on a leash. She plopped down on the side walk in front of my mother's house and refused to move. With a twinkle in her eye, Mochi's mischievous spirit was coming through.

Mochi was also very frail at this time, weighing around eight pounds while looking very thin. Her low weight made it very easy for me to take control of the situation by picking her up. Not all our future power struggles would be as easily resolved.

At the time, I had a very narrow view of animal communication. My understanding of animal communication was simple: the person or master tells the dog or servant what to do. It was the dog's job to obey. I thought that my job was to learn how to take control and give commands.

I really had no concept of the level of a dog's intelligence or even a clear understanding of how a dog takes in information. I accepted the common belief that a dog's primary sense is smell, with sight and hearing as secondary senses.

At that time I was quite comfortable with concepts of sensory perception, energy movement and telepathy but I never connected those theories to animals.

It was only in the writing of this little book did I discover more about Woodhouse's beliefs and practices. At an early age she had a tremendous love of animals, especially horses. After obtaining a basic education, not doing well at school, she managed to obtain an opportunity to live on an "estancia" or cattle farm in Argentina in the 1930's.

She had tremendous confidence in her ability to communicate with horses, developing a communication technique of breathing up the horse's nose. She would let the horse approach her while gently breathing down her own nostrils. When the horse was close enough, she would allow the animal to sniff her and blow up her nose. She would do the same in return, promoting a kind of mutual "nice to meet you" to gain their trust.

In her 1970 autobiography, *Talking to Animals*, Woodhouse tells of learning this method from a "Guarani Indian". Guarani, she describes, is a peaceable South American Indian Tribe living mainly in countries such as Paraguay, Uruguay and the Brazilian coast.

However, Woodhouse warns that this breathing method does not work the same for dogs since dogs know friend or foe by scent and *instinct.* Dogs also determine much information by tone of voice, preferring a more high pitched sound.

Bonding to Mochi Introduces Telepathy

She also points out that telepathy occurs easily from living closely with your animal. Considering that dogs and cats usually, share or in my case, dominate the household, what could be more natural than telepathy? So much information was available about animal communication and telepathy, but I was still blindsided.

Fortunately for both Mochi and myself, her clever personality shown through the haze of my understanding and helped resolve or, should I say, create many amusing if not precarious situations.

My mother immediately bonded with Mochi. However, bonding with my pet was not immediate for me. Later in the same day, after I visited my mother in Holmdel, I took Mochi to my home in Princeton.

She was a very awkward puppy and could not navigate the stairs to my backyard. Outside my backdoor is a high brick vintage 1949 deck with a wrought iron open railing and four deep brick steps. She could pull herself up, but could not walk down the steps. Maybe her front shoulders were not developed enough yet or maybe she didn't have the rhythm of moving her body, but she learned in days.

During our house training journey, I would guide her down the stairs to my back yard on the brown leash and encourage her to do "quickie". Without regrets, I chose the house training method of "crating" her.

One theory of crating is that an animal will keep the immediate living area clean and not urinate or defecate in the crate. The goal is for the dog to want to leave the crate to conduct her business, allowing the living area inside the crate to be kept clean. The beauty of this system is that any accidents will occur in the crate, not on the kitchen floor. Mochi used the crate successfully.

For several days, upon first coming home, I took her outside about every two to three hours around the clock. As time went on, I allowed her to walk about in the kitchen when I was home. Accidents did happen on the kitchen floor. We had no communication pattern. If she was sending any messages, I did not understand her messages of wanting to go out. The whole house training process took about eight months. She developed a feeling of safety in the crate.

Although the house training plan was a success, it had many setbacks. Just when I thought she was holding her water, I would let her out of her crate and then it would happen!

"Oh, no! You didn't! Not again!"

I watched as urine made its way through the groves of the tile on my kitchen floor. Frantically, I would try to mop it up before it

Bonding to Mochi Introduces Telepathy

could travel under my antique 1952 Tappan stove, the centerpiece of my kitchen. At one point my neighbor laughingly told me she could hear me screaming and yelling in desperation.

Bonding took an unexpected turn when my little dog had to go on our first visit to the veterinarian. Mochi was home with me less than a week when of course she coughed up a huge white green glob of mucous. The owner of the pet shop had mentioned that this might happen to Mochi, despite the antibiotic treatment to her kennel cough. She had said, if Mochi coughed up copious amounts of mucous, I should take action.

Not sure of what action I was supposed to take, I called the pet shop who advised me to take her to the veterinarian associated with the store. Back into the tiny carrying case she went and off we drove to an established veterinary clinic near the pet shop.

By this time I was a little fed up with the whole dog ownership, or should I say puppy ownership, role. In the middle of the night, my sleep was interrupted to take her out to conduct her business, not to mention taking her out every few hours during the day, as well as cleaning her crate, mixing her food and giving her constant attention.

I never forgot the look on the vet tech's face when he opened the back door of my black

Mazda sedan. When he saw a puppy inside the travel carrying case, he said "darling". A big, awkward looking, middle-aged man, he became very gentle when he lifted up my "darling." Suddenly, I felt a little less fed up with my dog person or adopted "motherhood" role.

The veterinary technician carried the travel case with my puppy into the building to an examining room where the veterinarian was stationed. The young veterinarian was a studious looking man. He examined Mochi and determined she still had kennel cough. After prescribing another round of antibiotics, the vet went on to explain that canine diseases are generally not contagious to humans, except possibly, if a human had a very poor functioning immune system, or was on chemotherapy.

The vet seemed to have sympathy for me and without my asking, wrote an "unfit for sale" letter. This document states that my little puppy was too sick to have been sold and forced the pet store to be responsible for any veterinary care my puppy might need.

In situations like this New Jersey law outlines consumer options to include returning the animal for a refund, keeping the animal and attempt to cure it, or return the animal and receive an animal or equal value. Without fully understanding or reflecting on these issues, I was choosing the second option-keeping my puppy and trying to make her well.

The letter was a great financial help for me, letting me be more confident when considering obtaining medical treatment. I did not have to weigh the treatment against what I would have to pay, as I do now with all our visits.

Finance and medical treatment are very tricky. I love Mochi and always consider her well-being, while at the same time I consider the cost. Her comfort needs to be separated from mine. Am I treating her for her benefit or mine? Is the treatment necessary? If drugs are being ordered, are they appropriate for the problem? How do they work chemically? What are their side effects? Is the least amount of medicine being prescribed that can solve the problem? If laboratory tests are being offered are the tests related to the problem? Is the veterinarian taking advantage of my affection for my dog?

Being a registered nurse really helps me answer the questions regarding necessary tests, treatment and drugs. Although I don't have professional experience in veterinary medicine, knowledge of drug chemistry and the vocabulary to read about drug action, laboratory tests and treatment is invaluable.

Our second visit to a veterinarian would come soon, this time closer to home.

What My Dog Told Me About Healthy Eating

Every July I make a trip to Wildwood, New Jersey to visit my Texan friends, the family that I was with when Mochi was born. Every year my friends travel to Wildwood to visit other members of their family. Wildwood is three hours from Princeton, so I drive down for an overnight trip.

Where would I leave Mochi while I was away from home? I couldn't leave her at a kennel since most kennels don't take puppies and on top of that she was contagious. Against my better judgment I took her back to the pet store. They agreed to keep her overnight. When I returned from Wildwood, I picked up Mochi and took her home. I soon realized that she was not doing well.

By this time we were not obligated to see the veterinarian associated with the pet shop, so I took her to a clinic that was five minutes from my house. Having a veterinarian close by comes in handy when your pet is not feeling well and does not want to travel. The practice was called 'The Princeton Veterinary Group". Consistent with the name of the practice, the lead vet, a man perhaps in his fifties, appeared very intelligent.

After listening to Mochi's lungs with his stethoscope, he felt that although she might still have kennel cough it had not traveled to her lungs. He also felt Mochi's belly and determined she had "giardia", a highly contagious stomach

Bonding to Mochi Introduces Telepathy

parasite. Contagious to dogs, this parasite was also contagious to humans. Additionally, he thought Mochi caught it at the pet store while I was sunning in Wildwood.

"How contagious is she?" I asked.

"Just use good hand washing technique," the vet answered.

One of the symptoms of giardia is diarrhea. I worked very hard at keeping Mochi's bowel movements in her crate. When she had an accident on my tile floor, I felt very uneasy and thoughts went through my mind as to whether I should continue ownership?

"What would happen if I returned her to the pet shop now?" I asked a friend who had owned many dogs and even breed some Siberian huskies.

"They'd probably put her down," she said without hesitation. I never thought about returning her again.

Mochi was a good patient and never complained about being sick. She was very quiet and just laid still or slept. I used to pick her up, place her in my lap and sing a lullaby to the tune of Rock a Bye Baby:

"Rock a bye kennel in the tree top.

What My Dog Told Me About Healthy Eating

When the wind blows the kennel will rock.

When the bow breaks the kennel will fall.

And down will come Mochi, kennel and all."

She seemed to enjoy being in my lap but I can't say she enjoyed my singing.

 I could not always tell if her health was improving. Weight gain was the easiest thing to notice since I picked her up a lot. She always felt so heavy, but she looked like skin and bones. I could feel her ribs, but not see them protruding from her fur- a good sign. If she were malnourished her ribs would be able to be seen as well as felt with my hand. We just stayed on the usual simple schedule of eating, crating, petting, singing and walking her in the back yard on a leash.

 Summer was peaking, and I had planned to attend an alternative health "dream" workshop in upstate New York. Mochi did not seem dramatically improved, so I was surprised when the veterinarian took a blood test which came back negative for giardia.

 A doggy day care operation was located in the basement of the veterinary clinic so Mochi stayed there while I went happily to my weekend workshop. Learning about interpreting dreams would add another dimension to my alternative health experiences as a Therapeutic Touch

Bonding to Mochi Introduces Telepathy

practitioner. Therapeutic Touch is a method that uses the hands to move the universal energy. Later I'll explain how this technique helped me with communicating with Mochi.

When I returned from my weekend workshop, Mochi seemed to be progressing nicely. Her daily routine included walks around the neighborhood, running around in the kitchen, confinement in the crate and being tied outside to an old clothesline stake. My back yard was yet to be fenced in. The only communication I was interested in was to know when she had to go out to conduct business.

Our third visit to the vet was for neutering. My back yard was not fenced in until Mochi was a little over a year old. Until the fence arrived, our outdoor routine included tying Mochi to the iron banister at the bottom of a small stone deck in the rear of my house. I would usually go into the house while she conducted her business. At one point, I gave her a medium sized raw carrot while I tied her to the banister and then went into the house. She seemed to like the carrot and I assumed she would eat it or leave it on the ground. When I returned it was gone.

Maybe a week later, Mochi had to go to the veterinarian to be neutered. I had strict instructions from the vet's office that after midnight, she was not to eat or drink. Or in

What My Dog Told Me About Healthy Eating

medical talk, she was NPO, the Latin abbreviation non per omni, nothing by mouth. Well of course the instructions weren't given to Mochi who didn't understand English let alone Latin. She only knew on this particular day, the day of the procedure, her person was not feeding her. At least that is what I thought at the time. Preparing to go to the vet's office, I tied her to the banister outside, so she could conduct her usual business or "quickie."

I went inside the house only to return in a few minutes to see her with a carrot in her mouth. Immediately I knew where it had come from. Since it was morning and she had not received her usual meal, she was hungry. What more natural thing to do than retrieve emergency food? Not only did she remember where she left her carrot, but I truly believe she understood what was going to happen to her. She was going to be taken somewhere she did not want to go to, to the vet. I quickly grabbed the carrot before she swallowed it, resolving not to tell the vet. Otherwise he might call off the procedure.

Mochi learned quickly that her dog person, me, would aggressively take things out of her mouth that she wanted to keep in there. I did not realize at the time how much I did not know. The neutering procedure went well. The carrot had caused no ill effects.

Bonding to Mochi Introduces Telepathy

However the veterinarian wanted to keep Mochi overnight in his clinic. It was part of the normal neutering procedure. Since no veterinary staff worked in the clinic overnight, I feared Mochi would be frightened if she were left alone. My little puppy looked so uncomfortable sitting in a small cage. If only she could talk to me. If only I could tell her what the plan was, that I would be back tomorrow to take her home.

I would not have been so upset if I had realized that Mochi did know what the plan was, just as she had known that we were going to the vet.

The one thing I did realize that day was that we had bonded. The vet tech in this veterinary hospital seemed indifferent to my concerns. The vet tech looked at me when I hesitated to leave my puppy. The expression on her face said I was over reacting, but I felt my behavior was reasonable. I was aware of how concerned I was about Mochi's feelings and well-being. I did not want to be separated from my little "darling."

One of Mochi's first days at home, while recovering from kennel cough.

Credit: Mary Ann Cavallaro

Chapter 3

Display Animals

What you see is not always what you get.

"One day we will see our animals again in the eternity of Christ. Paradise is open to all God's creatures."

Attributed to Pope Francis 2014

Originally spoken by Blessed Pope Paul VI (1963-78)

For the next several years, I looked at animals differently. From pets to farm animals, to animals in the wild, even to fish in the sea, I gave their plight a little more thought.

    I also became aware of Mochi's reaction to other animals. Although generally she did not seem disturbed by animals slightly larger than herself, having played with neighborhood labs, occasionally she had an unfavorable reaction.

Each Christmas season, the church I attended constructed a nativity scene. The staff built a wooden manger, added stone statues and brought in several farm animals including two donkeys, lambs, goats and several chickens. This living manger, in the tradition of St. Francis of Assisi, took place on the lawn in front of the rectory where the pastor lived.

The animals brought the scene to life. For me, the arrival of the animals was one of the highlights of the Christmas season. However, the animals were housed in a temporary wooden shed with a roof, with only plastic strips for a door. Not very much protection from New Jersey winters that can be very cold. On one occasion I took Mochi to visit this temporary pen.

When Mochi saw the large donkeys, she pulled back on her leash, refusing to go up to the fence that surrounded the pen. On the other side of the fence, the chickens, seeing the nearby dog, headed for shelter in their temporary shed, franticly banding together and clucking all the way home. It was our first and last visit to the living manger scene.

Perhaps because the living manger was part of a tradition that was in place before our pastor arrived, he endured this visiting troupe of

Display Animals

animals with a good nature. I remember the pastor saying in a sermon, "I know it is Christmas, because I can hear the rooster crowing." Not only did our pastor have a great sense of humor, but he had a chocolate lab, Toby, whom he loved.

On one particular Christmas when the animals arrived, for his dog's amusement and perhaps his own, he allowed his dog to run loose in the pen of the newly arrived visitors.

In his sermon, the priest merrily told how Toby chased the animals around the pen causing tremendous turmoil - knocking over statues, chasing animals fearing for their life, but of course not hurting anyone. Needless to say, the congregation had a great laugh.

Not everyone may have been laughing, because several years later at the start of the Christmas season, the pen was constructed, as usual, but the animals never arrived and never returned again. I suspect our pastor, as well as Toby, took this in stride without too much disappointment.

The visiting animal scene was always a highlight of the Christmas season for me. When it was removed, even though I missed it, I felt it was the right thing to do. There are so many other Christmas scenes to enjoy that do not involve live animals. The church continued to display beautiful statues of the nativity scene.

Farm animals on display in close, cold quarters caused justifiable complaints. The question also loomed in the background as to whether these animals lived out their normal life span. Visually it was difficult to determine this. Neither the donkeys nor the sheep looked terribly old. The sheep especially did not seem to age each year. The number of animals always remained basically the same. Were the animals neutered? If not, what happened to their offspring? Were the offspring sold as display animals or as meat?

You might want to think about these questions, especially the last one if you visit a "living history" farm or any other place that displays farm animals.

Another event at church was the blessing of the animals on the Feast of St. Francis of Assisi on October 4th. Mochi and I attended annually. Many Christian churches celebrate this feast day in early October during the wonderful weather of early fall. Members of the community are invited to bring their companion animal or perhaps a horse, depending on the community, to their respective churches for the minister to bless.

Display Animals

    At my church, on Nassau Street in Princeton, this event took place on the lawn . The lawn was bordered by hedges so the dogs, cats and occasional rabbits were conveniently separated from the sidewalk and Nassau Street. My church's ceremony included a guitarist who played while the community sang.

We also prayed the Prayer of St Francis:

Lord, make me an instrument of your peace.

Where there is hatred, let me sow love;

Where there is injury, pardon;

Where there is doubt, faith;

Where there is despair, hope;

Where there is darkness, light;

And where there is sadness, joy.

O Divine Master; Grant that I may not so much seek to be consoled as to console;

To be understood as to understand;

To be loved as to love;

For it is in giving that we receive;

What My Dog Told Me About Healthy Eating

It is in pardoning that we are pardoned;

And it is in dying that we are born to Eternal Life.

Toby's person, our pastor, had a lovely way of conducting the service. First he sang, prayed and blessed the animals in a group. Then he went around to each animal and its person and blessed the individual animal. I always remember the intent but happy look on our pastor's face when he dropped holy water on my little dog. I felt so happy!

A kindly parishioner usually attended to Toby while our pastor was occupied. Toby, tail wagging, joined in the fun.

Mochi was one and a half years old when she was blessed for the first time. She seemed only slightly ill at ease with the small crowd of animals and their people. Planning ahead I had taken my camera. When I saw a nearby man, I asked him to snap a picture of me and Mochi. He quickly obliged. Handing me back my camera, he said, "It's a nice one."

The picture turned out so well, I used it on my Christmas card that year. The photography shop that created the cards put it in their display of what a really good card looked like. This card started my annual tradition of putting Mochi's picture on my Christmas cards.

Display Animals

As she got older, whenever we attended the animal blessing event, she became very fearful and would pull on her leash so hard she nearly brought me to the ground. When she reached 11, rather than go to the St Francis event, I had her blessed privately by a family friend who was a priest on his annual visit to Princeton. When my priest friend no longer visited the area, at the suggestion from my parish bulletin, I recited some prayers and blessed her myself. It was not as much fun as the event at church, but I felt it still did Mochi some good. At the same time it became very glaring to me, that blessing your pet was not synonymous with having respect for all God's creatures.

All the while, I was monitoring the bond I had with my dog, I felt we had a good bond, but nothing more than any other responsible dog owner, or should I say crazy dog owner would have.

Our second annual Christmas card

Credit: Picture was taken by an unknown passerby.

Chapter 4

Mochi Goes to Syracuse and Uses Her Instincts

"You can bring Mochi too," my longtime friend Bob said when he invited me to travel with him to visit his twin sister, Sue, who lived in Syracuse, New York. Sue was also a close friend of mine. Since Bob had pet sat with Mochi a couple of years before, they had developed quit a friendship.

During the summer of 2003, Bob, Mochi and I set off for Syracuse. Mochi's usual mode of transportation was a bed in the cargo area of my Volvo wagon with a screen separating her from the passenger seat.

Sue's neighborhood always caused me a great deal of concern. She lived in the same house she grew up in with her parents and her brother. The building, a Victorian style two family house, was originally in a good neighborhood. Over the years after her parents died, the neighborhood severely deteriorated. Although Sue insisted that said she had wonderful neighbors, both Bob and I repeatedly tried to persuade her to move. She would not listen to either of us.

Bob and Sue's family had lived in the lower level of the house with relatives living on the upper level. Careers took both Bob and Sue out of upstate New York, but when their parents became elderly, Sue moved back to New York to take care of them.

Since the relatives had vacated years earlier, Sue moved into the upstairs apartment of her parent's old house, while her parents lived downstairs. After the death of Bob and Sue's parents, Sue lived in this fairly large house alone. Our plan was to stay in this house during our visit to Syracuse.

After a relaxing ride upstate, we approached Sue's neighborhood, driving through what looked a great deal like an inner city neighborhood. I noticed pit bulls in several of the backyards.

As Sue welcomed us into the house, I had a feeling of going back in time. The lower half of the house was virtually untouched since the parents had departed. The vintage dining room set was intact; her mother's dishes from the 1940s were displayed in a corner glass china cabinet. The kitchen had an original Formica counter with a Magic Chef stove standing against the wall. It gave me an eerie feeling.

Bob wanted to let Mochi have run of the house. However, since Mochi was not used to wide open spaces in a strange place and she never liked climbing up and down stairs, I decided to crate her in a downstairs bedroom. She would stay in the crate while we were out and during the night.

Territorial rights in the house were very relaxed. Bob decided to sleep in a bedroom in the downstairs apartment where he had grown up. Having redone her upstairs apartment, Sue wanted me to sleep in an upstairs' bedroom. I agreed.

The first night of our visit, I had difficulty sleeping because I could hear loud voices coming from outside in the neighborhood. It seemed like the noise was coming from the house next door to us.

Waking up very early, I went down stairs to see how Mochi was doing. After taking Mochi outside to do her business, since it was quiet and neither Bob nor Sue was up yet, I let Mochi loose in the house.

She went into the living room, looked up and stared out of a side window. She growled. It was only the second time I had ever heard her growl. Quickly I went over and looked out the window only to see a woman standing on the porch of a house two houses down. She was stocky and had black curly hair. By this time Sue was awake. We discussed the night noise. She said a neighbor was having a party. She liked all her neighbors, except this one troublesome neighbor who had the noisy party.

"Which house does she live in?" I asked.

"The house two houses down from mine," Sue answered, pointing in the direction Mochi had growled at.

"The house with the porch?"

"Yes."

"Is your neighbor stocky and does she have curly black hair?"

"Yes. How did you know?" Sue looked puzzled.

Sue wasn't the only one who was puzzled. Somehow Mochi knew this lady was not a nice lady.

Chapter 5

Down on a Grass-Fed Cattle Farm

"The fact is, a cow always knows which calf is hers."

Howard Lyman, the mad cowboy, 2006

Mad cow was raging in the United States and England in January 2004. The virus known as Bovine Spongiform Encephalopathy (BSE) caused 4.4 million cows to be put down in the United Kingdom during the eradication period. The US general public cut back on meat consumption. This twist of circumstance helped the local cattle farmer.

Consumers concerned about their health were tremendously interested in local farmers raising grass fed-cattle. These cattle farmers generally have no need to give their animals antibiotics since there is no overcrowding. Neither do they have the need to give them hormones, thereby allowing them to grow at normal rates and weight.

As a freelance writer for our local Princeton newspaper, I was always thinking up story ideas. I had become a writer to promote my entrepreneurial ventures. As my own dietary habits changed, my articles reflected the change, but I never liked frightening people into not eating meat.

Being a vegetarian, I had no worries personally about so called mad cow and I thought an article about this issue was timely. This being a controversial subject, making fewer writers wanting to tackle it, may have helped to get my article published.

One of my entrepreneurial ventures was to become an organic herb farmer, or rather gardener, developing one quarter acre plot located in back of my mother's house. During this brief excursion in the organic world, one of my contacts gave me the name of the manager of a grass-fed cattle farm several miles from my house in Princeton.

The manager of the farm seemed a bit hesitant to grant an interview, explaining he was really in the meat industry and did not want to deter people from eating meat. When I reassured him that the article would focus on the more humane aspects of how he raised his cattle rather than on the evils of factory farming, he agreed.

On the appointed day, leaving now three year old Mochi sleeping snuggly in the kitchen, I drove the four miles to his farm in Princeton, just beyond the center of town. A recent snow storm made this cold day in January even more difficult to get around in.

Turning into the long farmhouse driveway, it felt strange to see cows in the upscale area of Princeton, New Jersey. But when the farmer opened the door of his old farmhouse and invited me in to sit in a cozy room with a wood burning stove, everything began to feel natural.

In an attempt to find common ground, I opened the discussion with "Since mad-cow is such an issue, I thought it would be good to understand the alternative method that you use of raising cattle."

He seemed to like this approach and began talking easily about how he raised his cattle feeding them grass from the pasture where they naturally grazed, rather than grain. "The cows take care of themselves. There is no need to pick up their manure. It nourishes the land."

At this point in our conversation, I felt it was necessary to clarify my feelings about cattle. Not wanting to bring up the treatment of animals, I explained I became a vegetarian for "health reasons." This was the truth, since in those days I had little understanding of the factory farming of animals. A troubled expression came over his face when I explained this. It was not clear to me whether he was frowning about my health issue or my negativity toward eating meat, but never the less, I felt a little warmer towards him.

My limited understanding of the concentration camp like conditions animals are raised in may have been related to denial. In the case of animal consumption, it never occurred to me to find out more. If I investigated further where the meat I had eaten came from, I may have felt guilty. At this time, I had been a vegetarian for only five years.

The farm is not very visible from the road. When I mentioned that many times when I drove by in the past I could not see any cows, he explained that he rotates the cows from front pastures to back pastures. The farm covers approximately 125 acres. Many times driving by I observed the cows and their young calves comfortably grouped in small herds in the roomy pasture, never crowed.

Down on a Grass-Fed Cattle Farm

I was surprised and disturbed when he told me that that his average cow, whose normal life span is 10 to 12 years, is killed at 18 months. In people years, if we use the seven year axiom used for dogs, that amounts to killing a 10 year old with a life span of 84 years.

The farmer recounted his work history as growing up on a dairy farm with the dream of someday managing his own farm. He found raising a family difficult as a dairy farmer. His wife worked as well. He felt very grateful for having the opportunity to manage the Princeton farm.

At the time of our interview, he had only managed the farm for one year. Although he expressed a great passion for his work with the cows and confidence in himself, he did not appear overly sure that grass-fed farm concept would be a success.

His fears were unfounded. With the public's interest in avoiding hormones and antibiotics, grass-fed cattle became popular.

Approximately 10 years later, when the Princeton farm was touted as a model grass-fed cattle operation, I heard the same farmer speak at an environmental event. I was surprised to hear him mention that he had worked three years in pig confinement or the factory farming of pigs.

What My Dog Told Me About Healthy Eating

I heard him speak on two different occasions. The first time he appeared almost boastful, ludicrously describing, some of his adventures in this horrific environment such as removing injured or dead pigs through some sort of a chute.

On the second occasion he appeared more somber with an almost saddened expression when he said this was "a job" he did for three years in order to help feed his family. The sponsor of these events portrayed him as coming a long way, from factory farming pigs in concentration camp like conditions, to raising pigs in a pastoral setting.

It made me stop and think about my experience with a pig when I was a little girl. Whenever I think about the incident, I wonder why it took me so long to raise my consciousness.

Little Jimmy grazing safely at Skylands Animal Sanctuary.

Credit: Mary Ann Cavallaro

Chapter 6

My Father, Myself

My father was born in southern Italy during the early 1900s. When he was a young boy living in the extremely rural Southern Italian town of Nardodipace, it was common to raise a family pig and then kill it and eat it.

In Italy, as well as in the United States in the early 1900s, supermarkets as we know them today did not exist. The majority of family food was obtained from the field and farm animals.

My father came to the United States when he was 19, working as a coal miner in a Virginia coal mine, as a migrant worker on a vegetable farm, a worker in a cork factory and finally as a janitor in a school. For the first few years of my life which I vaguely remember, my brother and I lived with my parents in a few rented rooms upstairs in a house in a small rural community.

At that time my father worked in a factory, and with help from my grandfather, he was able to buy five acres of property in the same town. Together they built a small house on the property. When my father wasn't working in the factory, he indulged in his passion of farming. He followed the practices he was familiar with in Italy, growing fruits, wonderful strawberries and vegetables.

At one point my father bought a goat for its milk to make goat cheese, a favorite of his. He tied the black and white goat on a leash and connected the leash to a stake in the front of the house. Someone from the SPCA or other animal protection agency rightfully complained. The goat disappeared.

A little later my father was able to buy a pig and raise it in an enclosed pen in the back of our house, the pigpen. His goal was just as it was in Italy: raise the pig and slaughter it for family food. I never fed the pig or cleared away its waste. My father was the major care taker.

I remember someone came out to give it shots, perhaps deworming medicine. My father was on top of everything where the pig was concerned. I was impressed with my father when he went to the neighbor who bordered our back yard and offered him some bacon in return for the neighbor not making any official complaints. It may not have been acceptable even back then in the 50s to suddenly raise a pig when no live stock had been on the property in the past.

Although more intelligent than even dogs, pigs are socially less acceptable than even goats.

As a little girl I watched the pig grow but never really bonded with it as a pet. We never gave the pig a name. I vaguely remember my parents discussing the slaughter of the pig. The event was not something that my brother and I were actively included in. On the appointed day one or two men came and, together with my father, they went about their job. My mother, my brother and I were in the background watching. The men seemed to have a hard time tackling the pig even in the small space of the pigpen. I remember they finally cornered him up against the wire fence that enclosed the pen. I vividly recall the scene and vaguely remember the pig grunting, but I have no recollection of how they killed the animal or seeing the animal dead.

The men seemed serious and determined to do the job with no jubilation. There was no sympathy for the animal. It seemed expected that the animal's job was to die. While at the same time, they must have been very aware that the pig was terrified because he reacted fearfully, as if they were going to hurt him.

Unfortunately, my conscience was not working as well as Donald Watson, the creator of veganism. After watching a pig being slaughtered on his grandfather's farm where he was visiting when he was a boy, Watson stopped eating animals forever.

Why tell this story about the pig? Why talk about my father? I'm sharing the story about the pig and my father to explain that I loved my father the way he was. Coming from where he did and his life experiences only gave him so many options. Understanding his experiences gives me a little more insight to understanding his choices as well as mine.

Sometimes my friends are uncomfortable when eating meat in front of me. Maybe they feel they are being offensive to me? Maybe they feel guilty? Perhaps they feel they are being judged or that I harbor anger towards them? It is a subject I find hard to discuss with friends or family. Timing is important. During a meal when another is eating a steak may not be the best time to discuss cattle torture.

The ease of discussion also bears a direct connection to the strength of the relationship with friend or family. An open mind on both sides is helpful here, as well as a comfort level with discussing a subject with conflicting viewpoints. In order to understand the other's position, try to understand the thoughts and feelings of the person you are communicating with who does not share your views.

My Father, Myself

It is interesting to note here that although Woodhouse and Watson each grew up in the same rural area of the United Kingdom, and during the same time period, their experiences and beliefs were different. Born in England in 1910, the same year as Barbara Woodhouse, Watson stopped eating meat as a New Year's resolution when he was 14 years old. He continued to drink milk.

Woodhouse seemed to classify her horses and dogs as "pets" making it OK to slaughter cattle and other farm animals for food. Watson moved away from eating farm animals since it caused them pain and suffering. Although he initially drank milk he chooses not to after further insight into the milk production industry of his time. He stopped drinking milk in the 1940s.

Woodhouse milked cows daily for a supply of milk for family and for sale. To her credit she treated her farm animals well while they were in her possession. However, she made little attempt to let them live out their natural life span. Also to her credit, she fought tirelessly for gentler approaches to horse training, promoting techniques she learned while living in Argentina.

In Watson's case he was able to go several steps further than Woodhouse, my father or myself. Even with the limited choices of his times, he was affected when he saw how eating animals caused pain and suffering, and he changed his behavior.

If you are thinking of changing your diet, it is good to note that even the father of veganism made his dietary change gradually. Watson's behavior change was thought out and took some time.

Initially Watson was not a "vegan" or someone who uses no animal products such as meat, milk, eggs and fish. He moved away from dairy or milk only after several years of not eating meat.

I feel sometimes people try to make changes that are too much and too soon. Watson had an emotional reaction to the killing of the pig, but he also had a carefully thought out plan for change. For lasting success in dietary change, it seems conscious effort needs to accompany the emotional motivator.

In his book, *Change of Heart*, Nick Cooney notes that people, who change their diets because of compassion to animals, rather than health reasons, remain on their meatless diets longer.

My own nursing background has given me many opportunities to observe people making decisions about their dietary habits. It always mystifies me when patients with the same diagnosis or similar health circumstances, make radically different decisions about their diets.

Many times people who are newly diagnosed with cancer, kidney disease or heart disease are motivated to adopt vegan diets while others make little if no change.

Even being a nurse and feeling compassion for people, it took some time to feel compassion for farm animals. Initially changing my diet for health reasons, I gave no thought to animal suffering until I read Peter Singer's *Animal Liberation*. Rather than emotional sensationalism, his book gave me some objective facts. Today, if I was miraculously guaranteed no serious ailments and could die of old age peaceably, I would still never eat an animal.

How was I able to make the shift of motivation from personal health to compassion for animals? Peter Singer's book made a big impact, but I think I also had a little help from a friend.

My father is driving his tractor home after working in the fields next to our house.

Credit: Cavallaro Family

Chapter 7

Raising Cows and Sending Them to a Slaughter House

"Through pride we are ever deceiving ourselves. But deep down below the surface of the average conscience a still, small voice says to us, something is out of tune."
C.G. Jung, psychiatrist and psychotherapist (1876-1961)

I left the Princeton cow farm that cold January day not really sure what my story was about. But that is the way I write articles, not determining ahead of time what, if any, the angle of the story will be. Instead, I write the interview as it unfolds and then review what was said.

    I had lined up a second interview in the Princeton Area with another beef farmer and his wife who had a similar setup as the first beef farmer. In this case, the farmer and his wife owned their own grass-fed cattle enterprise rather than managed it, as did the first farmer.

This farm was on a side road making the animals less visible than the Princeton pastures.

As I drove up the driveway, I could see several cows in a pasture that led up to a re-built farm house. The farmer's wife invited me into their warm cozy kitchen, where I waited with her and their friendly dog for the farmer to arrive for our interview.

In conversation, the wife revealed that she and her husband had recently lost a child and she found farming comforting. The young woman exuded peacefulness as she sat across the table from me. Her husband brought in equally good energy when he entered the room to begin our interview.

Unlike the first farmer who had worked in the meat industry, this farmer had owned a heating and air conditioning company prior to buying his farm. Originally, he planned his venture to be a chicken farm. Unfortunately, although both husband and wife each worked very hard in the chicken industry, their enterprise did not prove successful. "We couldn't make any money," the husband stated.

They based their entry into the meat industry on their dislike of meat in the supermarket. "My son thought it tasted terrible," said the farmer. They bought two cows for their own personal consumption. Since they had the property, they began raising cattle.

The man smiled as he talked a little about his neighbors. One neighbor whom he referred to as an "old timer" liked to check up on any of the cows that had physical problems. He formed an attachment to them, even though the cattle were headed for slaughter,

The wife described her husband's disgust when the butcher from the slaughter house used an electric cow prod to move the cows into the van that would transport the cows to their death. Even though they had formed some bonds to the cows, they were able to send them to be killed.

"We got over our feelings," she said.

Listening to this surprised me. It was the first time I had ever heard anyone discuss this. I was surprised that they had feelings of remorse and even more surprised that they went on with the activity, if they felt the way they did. At the time, however, I wasn't curious enough to explore her feelings.

Looking back, I realized I missed a big opportunity to gain more understanding about these feelings. Maybe I did not ask any questions since my article was not going to be about killing farm animals or maybe my consciousness hadn't been raised yet.

What My Dog Told Me About Healthy Eating

Chapter 8

The Look in the Eye

"If slaughterhouses had glass walls, the whole world would be vegetarian."

Linda McCartney (1941-1998)

I put all my notes together and wrote the article for the Princeton Packet Business Journal. It maintained that, for health and humane reasons, it was better to eat grass-fed rather than factory farmed beef. It made the cover of the journal.

Needless to say the newspaper got several nasty "letters to the editor" from vegetarians. One letter criticized how I described the family living on the farm as being "in harmony with nature." Looking back, I have to admit it was a just criticism. In 2004 killing animals that you've raised doesn't seem to be in harmony with many things.

The reaction did not trouble me too much. Several years before, a woman whom I had interviewed was outraged by an article I had written about vegetarian cooking. The woman wrote a letter to the editor saying that she was aghast that I included meat in a recipe. She felt betrayed. In this case, I felt the lady should have contacted me beforehand, in addition to writing to the editor. Neither of these reactions or the interviews seemed to open my mind as to my commitment to avoid eating meat.

My dog was three years old when I wrote this article in 2004. As she does to this day, Mochi sleeps through most of my writing. Since Mochi is afraid of heights and will not go upstairs where I have my home office, I solve the problem by writing downstairs. I place my computer on the kitchen table to write while Mochi snores gently, snuggled in her bed under an antique church pew.

Two years later The American Vegan Society asked me to do a book review and gave me a list of books to choose from. The list included Peter Singer's *In Defense of Animals*. I had heard Dr. Singer speak as a guest lecture at a global economics seminar I had attended on the Princeton University Campus. He greatly impressed me, so I chose his book to review. If you are not familiar with this man, his central concern is the ethics surrounding global as well as personal actions. Many of his books discuss the ethics involved in global poverty and handling of the environment. His positions on abortion and euthanasia often meet with much opposition. He was one of the first people to discuss the treatment of animals as an ethical matter. To give me a sense of history and prepare for the interview with this controversial figure, the *American Vegan* editor gave me a copy of Dr. Singer's first landmark book, *Animal Liberation*.

The book, relating stories of gruesome factory farming especially of cows and pigs, outraged me. The description of research involving chimpanzees and gorillas surprised me.

It was the end of 2005. At the time I read the book I was still eating fish and using animal products such as leather shoes and belts. I decided to use the momentum of the New Year and committed to no longer using any animal products and to become a complete vegan.

On the appointed day of the interview, March 31, 2006, I drove to the Princeton University campus to meet with Dr. Singer. At the time he was the Ira W. DeCamp Professor of Bioethics. Having read that he was considered by some to be among one of the ten greatest minds in the world, I decided I would not try to argue any points if I disagreed with him. Actually he seemed very comfortable with himself and even tried to help me explore some of my own statements in a supportive way.

With the start of many of my interviews, I try to find common ground. When I announced that I was a vegetarian and had changed my dietary habits because of health issues, it made little impression on him. When I confessed I attended thoroughbred horse races, he smiled and said that horse racing took up such a small percentage of animal abuse compared to his primary concern-factory farming of animals. Inadvertently, I had broken the ice.

The major reason he does not eat animals stems from the fact that animals feel physical pain and even emotional pain or anxiety. We talked a little about the difficulty of being a vegan in a predominately meat eating culture. Often when he traveled, he said that he found it very hard to eat a nutritious meal that did not include meat or dairy. During those times, he said he might eat some dairy.

"Being vegan is not a religion. I'm not a religious person."

He also added, we should not act self-righteous, but rather we should "be an example" and "be ready to talk about why we eat the way we do."

When we talked about the difficulty of finding the right image to capture the horrors of factory farming, he said something that always stands out vividly in my memory. He spoke with affection about how a colleague of his, Henry Spira, tried to get the point of animal cruelty across by creating a newspaper ad showing a hound dog in a frankfurter roll. Maybe the dog even had a little mustard on it. Instantly I saw Mochi on a hotdog roll.

The ad didn't work. It was not well received by the public who did not want to see a pet in a dangerous position. The public also did not make the connection between a dog and a factory farmed animal. Dogs are viewed as pets, while farm animals are viewed as food.

A picture of this ad appears in the book Singer wrote about his friend, Henry Spira. The book *Ethics into Action* is a short easy read about Spira's ground breaking animal rights initiatives during the 1970s. Spira's activism centered on the cosmetics industry where animals were tortured to test beauty products. His initiatives began the compassionate process of not testing on animals. Animals benefit from Spira's work today.

The interview ended on a positive note with Dr. Singer presenting me with his business card. The finished article appeared as a book review in the *American Vegan Magazine* 6-1, Summer 2006.

All this time, whenever I drove past the local grass-fed cattle farm, I looked for the cows.

What My Dog Told Me About Healthy Eating

One day, some months after that interview with Dr. Singer, I drove past the farm and saw a cow; I saw my Mochi's face on the cow. To this day, whenever I see an animal in a vulnerable position, I see my dog's face on it. I don't see Mochi's physical face with her long floppy ears, but I see the look in eye of the animal and it is if I am looking into Mochi's eyes. I don't usually do it consciously, it just happens.

My eating choices became very clear and also very simple. Of course, I would never do anything to hurt my Mochi, so therefore I would never do anything to hurt another animal. In the end, the way I choose to eat has become less related to my health and more related to compassion for animals.

Chapter 9

Talk to Me

"... I firmly believe that intuitive or symbolic sight is not a gift but a skill..."

Caroline Myss

Anatomy of the Spirit, 1996

About a year after the Singer interview, when Mochi was about 6 years old, we started visiting with an animal communicator who made promotional visits to our local pet store. The visit was prompted by Mochi's interaction with our neighbor's ferocious dog.

    A fence divided my neighbor's back yard from mine. When I took up residence in Princeton, the house directly behind me was owned by a doctor whose ex-wife lived in the house with Jake, a Golden Retriever.

Jake would come up to the fence and mingle with my little puppy through the wire. I felt Mochi thought Jake was her mother.

One day the woman, whom I had gotten to know and like, told me she and Jake were leaving because she could not afford the upkeep of this Princeton home. I felt very unhappy. Her ex-husband whom she described as not a "dog person" would be moving back in. Sadly Mochi and I said good-bye to Jake and his person.

For several years after they left, Mochi was still outgoing and playful, and still played happily in my backyard.

During one summer, I returned from my yearly July visit with Maria and her family in Wildwood and was dismayed to see a pit bull mix dog appear in this neighbor's yard. The doctor had a live-in house keeper who had rescued this misguided dog named, Lady. When Mochi first went up to Lady who stood behind the wire fence, perhaps thinking she was Jake, the mixed breed tried to bite Mochi through the fence.

Lady's usual routine was to run back and forth behind the fence all the while barking wildly. On her side of the fence Mochi would mirror her running, back and forth. The situation got decidedly worse when two of Lady's friends joined her. Mochi wanted friendship and in return got a pack of noisy aggressive dogs.

Mochi became withdrawn and fearful. She now backed away from larger breed dogs when previously she would playfully bound up to them. She also shied away from barking dogs and would not walk to the end of our yard to avoid meeting Lady and company.

When I saw an ad for an animal communicator, I wondered if she might be able to help me understand why Mochi's personality had changed.

The communicator, whom I will call Amethyst, concentrated and connected with Mochi. She then could tell me what Mochi was feeling in general. Or specifically, I would pose a question and she would ask Mochi the question and convey to me the dog's answer. I admit I went in skeptical, but she won me over on our first visit.

Sitting in a corner of the pet store, Amethyst, a very attractive red haired woman seemed unaware of the movement of the shoppers, dogs and store staff. When it was our turn, Mochi and I approached her. She offered me a seat in a folding chair near her. Mochi stood looking around.

Poised and centered, Amethyst totally focused on Mochi, closing her eyes and bowing her head for a few minutes to connect with the animal, while my dog sat at a distance not paying any attention to her.

Opening her eyes, she said, "Mochi is frightened by big dogs." This was not very new information and I was unimpressed. But when she imitated Lady, Amethyst threw an imaginary toy in the air and, with her fingers, flicked the imaginary toy around while even snarling a little with her mouth, I became a believer. I had seen Lady do this countless number of times!

Whenever Amethyst came to town Mochi and I would get an appointment. I still did not fully believe she was reading Mochi's mind. Rather I thought she might be reading my mind. But she was definitely connecting with someone!

Not only was Amethyst centered, but she spoke with caring in her soft voice. As I got to know her a little better we discussed her techniques. At Amethyst suggestion, I read J. Allen Boone's *Kinship with all Animals* and the communication process of animals fell into place.

Boone, a writer to begin with, tells his story of how he dog sat with a famous Hollywood German Shepard named Strongheart. Their meeting took place in the 1920s. Living with Strongheart, Boone came to realize the dog could read his mind.

Boone recounts how one day, sitting at his typewriter trying to write, he felt it was too beautiful a day to work but wanted the day off. He really had a strong desire to go for a walk. Suddenly Strongheart came up to him carrying his walking stick and then pulled out his hat and a pair of jeans. Boone believed Strongheart had read his mind and was preparing for the walk.

Kinship with all Animals is a short enjoyable book and highly recommended if you want to understand animals better. This field of animal communication, although not new, is growing in popularity. Telepathy, a method of mentally connecting with another in their presence or at a distance, is also not new.

Boone describes a communication bridge that can exist between humans and animals by consciously or unconsciously creating it. Initially with him as well as me, the bridge appeared unconsciously. We were talking and listening to our dogs before we even realized it. We were experiencing the telepathy of close quarters that Barbara Woodhouse described.

This type of communication reminded me of a complementary medical healing technique I had learned many years before called Therapeutic Touch. This technique can be used in close quarters with the subject in your physical presence, or with the subject at a distance.

What My Dog Told Me About Healthy Eating

Chapter 10

Therapeutic Touch Reaches Animal Communication

"If I can do it (perform Therapeutic Touch) you can too!"

Dolores Krieger at 1998 Conference in Pumpkin Hollow, NY

I first became acquainted with Therapeutic Touch approximately 35 years ago when I attended a nursing in-service. A nurse demonstrated the technique and told how she had used it to help heal her school age daughter's broken arm. Again this is another example of two people living in close proximity.

    This chapter may read more like instruction, but that is my intention. If you want to practice Therapeutic Touch or animal

83

communication techniques some concrete instruction is helpful.

Therapeutic Touch (TT) is a consciously directed method that uses the hands to move energy to cause relaxation. It is the relaxation that promotes the healing. It is based on the idea that a universal energy exists that sustains life. TT is a contemporary interpretation of several ancient healing practices.

My interpretation is that different Eastern cultures experience this same universal energy but give it their own cultural name. In India or Ayurvedic medicine the energy is "prana" or breath, in China it is "qi" or "chi "(pronounced chee) or universal force and in Japan it is the "yin" and the "yang", interconnected opposite forces.

Each of us, human and animal, has an energy field that radiates two or three inches from the body and interacts with the environment. The TT practitioner tunes into this energy field's subtle flow. When disease, injury or emotional distress is present, the flow is blocked. By moving her hand through the person or animal's energy field, the TT practitioner can sense the blockage and then rebalance the energy flow.

Two women, Dolores Krieger and Dora Kunz co-developed the Therapeutic Touch technique in 1972. Krieger is a registered nurse with a PhD and also a nursing professor at New York University, while Kunz possessed clairvoyant faculties. Together they made quite a team!

Kunz focused on the technique and medical diagnosis, while Krieger was instrumental introducing the technique into nursing circles. They have each written numerous books published in many languages. Krieger and Kunz were both firm believers that anyone could learn the technique of Therapeutic Touch. They clearly said they had no special powers.

Kunz was high spirited, always joking around while Krieger was mellower, but also had a good sense of humor. They worked together for over fifty years. They were also both dog lovers and vegetarians.

I learned the Therapeutic Touch technique from Dolores Krieger at a workshop she conducted in New York City. I didn't meet Kunz until later in 1998, when she and Krieger were conducting a workshop together. They were two of the first vegetarians I had ever met.

The week long workshop with Krieger and Kunz began in an old farm house in upstate NY. It was early evening and I vividly remember when I walked into the living room, noticing brochures depicting animal cruelty left out for view on some side tables. I looked away. The thought that went through my mind was that I just didn't want to deal with this. But what lingered in my mind was that these two women felt it was important to spread this information.

At that time I ate meat and gave some thought to diet change but did little about it. The workshop cafeteria served vegetarian meals which I was comfortable eating. This workshop at Pumpkin Hollow, Therapeutic Touch headquarters, was one of the last major conferences the duo conducted together. Dora van Gelder Kunz passed away in 1999 at the age of 95.

Several years later, I had the privilege of interviewing Dolores Krieger and subsequently wrote an article "The Legend of Pumpkin Hollow" which was published in *Nursing Spectrum* magazine on February 12, 2007. Krieger said that her friendship with Kunz began not for philosophical reasons, but for practical reasons: Kunz needed transportation to her sessions with doctors and clergy, and Krieger had a car.

The name Therapeutic Touch is a misnomer because the person or animal does not have to be touched or even present. The first step in the process is intentionality or having good will toward your subject. This step generally is not emphasized since the modality is based on the natural human potential to reach out in compassion and empathy and many times is performed in a healing environment. Compassion and empathy can be extended to humans or animals. However in today's complex society, I feel intentionality has become an important step.

The second step in the process is to center yourself or clear your mind. Centering is going within yourself to focus.

To deliver the technique with a person or animal in your presence, hands are held about an inch away from the surface of the subject's body, and then moved over the body surface sensing any irregular energy. Unbalanced energy may be sensed by the hand as static, pressure, or a decrease in pressure, experienced as suction or a pulling of the hand.

After performing this assessment, unruffle or break up the energy with a fluttering hand movement over the affected area or an associated area.

After unruffling, holding your hands just above the surface of the body, make quick sweeping movements along the body part you are working on, always sweeping in a downward direction. This sweeping movement moves the energy downward or with the natural gravity felt on the body. If you were working on a leg, you would start at the knee and stroke downward toward the ankle.

The final step is "grounding" or ending the energy flow. Usually this is done by gently wrapping your hands on the ankle or wrist after the last stroke of hand movement. If you were working on the knee, you would ground by gently but firmly taking hold of the ankle. After grounding, you could also go back and do another assessment to determine if the energy feels different or improved.

Being a TT practitioner for over 15 years, I also frequently used healing at a distance. In this case the person or animal is not present at the session. For healing at a distance, through imagery and visualization, the person or animal is pictured. Love or good will is sent to the subject. The sender or person initiating the thoughts visually pictures herself or himself performing Therapeutic Touch on the person or animal. Visualization is like a remote video.

One of the most amusing incidents for me of distance healing happened while working with a New Jersey friend who had recently moved to Rhode Island. She emailed that after the move her cat took sick and stopped eating. I tried TT at a distance and later my friend wrote that the same day I started the therapy, the cat began to eat. Was this coincidence? Seems she had swallowed a small ball of thread or wool.

Therapeutic Touch Reaches Animal Communication

The most amazing incident of TT on Mochi occurred when she had some sort of allergic skin condition. I had taken her to our veterinarian at the time, who prescribed cortisone tablets. It was late in the afternoon. I gave her the first dose at bedtime and then I too went up to bed. I was awakened several hours later by her pacing in the kitchen. She was restlessly pacing and shaking. Out of desperation I performed TT. Wondering what to do next, I was just about to give up when she calmed down, stepped into her bed, curled up and went to sleep.

Was this another coincidence? Maybe the medicine had begun to work. Maybe TT helped the medicine to work. Whatever the cause, Mochi's condition improved and I've used TT on her ever since.

When performing TT on Mochi while she is lying down, many times she will pick her head up or even move away. This might be her way of saying she is aware that something is happening. See what reaction your animal has. When using the technique on your animal for the first time or if your animal can be aggressive, take precautions. If she is physically present, play it safe and perform the action at a safe distance from your animal. Healing at a distance may be a better fit for an aggressive animal.

With a human, permission needs to be obtained from the subject before beginning Therapeutic Touch. When the animal is not yours, permission should first be obtained from the animal's person.

With an animal, obtaining permission is not as straight forward, but is just as important. Explaining what you intend to do may be helpful to you and the animal, even if you cannot perceive if the animal understands you.

With animal communication as well as TT, the first major step is to center yourself, clear your mind and relax. Have a positive attitude. The next steps are slightly different for animal communication than for performing TT.

Tell the animal how much you love her and that you want to connect. Open yourself to the universal energy flow. Merge with the animal. When you feel you have merged, pose your question and see if any thoughts or pictures come to mind. Are any feelings sensed? Follow your intuition. This process can be used whether the animal is physically with you or at a distance.

Performing TT gave me some help with learning animal communication. However each modality can be experienced or learned on its own. Perhaps you are using some energy method other than TT that can be a benefit to or adapted to animal communication

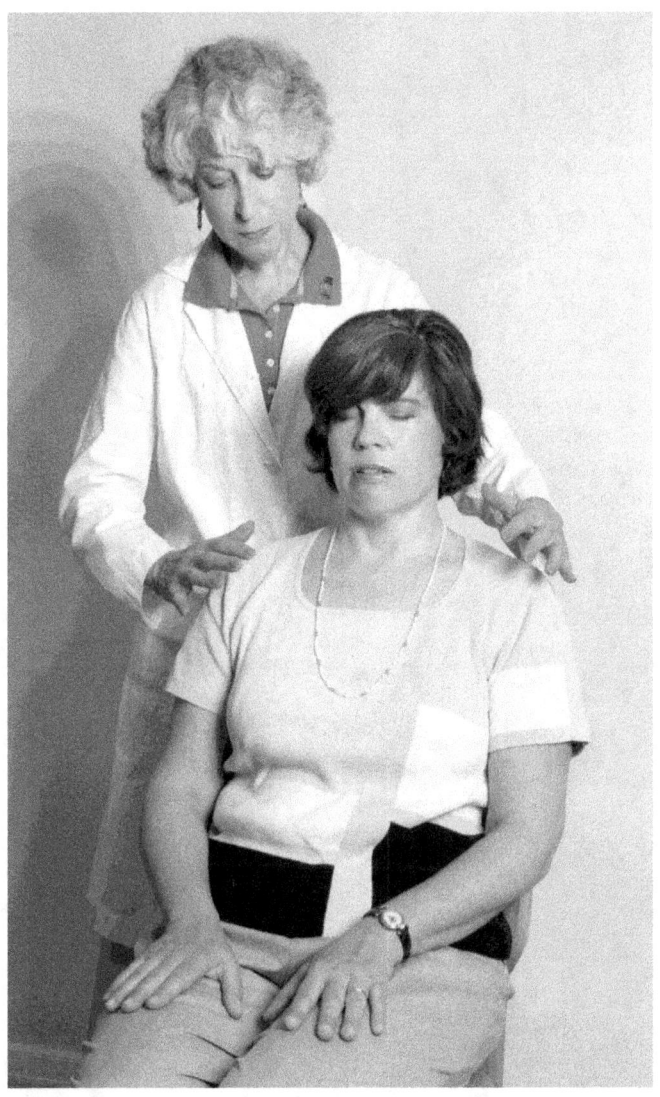

Diana, receiving TT from Mary Ann.

Credit: Frank Wojciechowski

What My Dog Told Me About Healthy Eating

Chapter 11

Chip, the Farm Dog

I wanted to experience more than the natural communication of close quarters or living with my animal. When Amethyst offered workshops in animal communication, I attended two basic sessions which reviewed the process described in a previous chapter. At the close of each session, in addition to our own pets, she suggested we practice on animals other than our own.

    Armed with an increase in knowledge and a corresponding increase in confidence, I approached a friend requesting to practice on her farm dog, Chip.

    For over 10 years I have been a member of Honeybrook Organic Farm, a community supported agriculture (CSA) farm in Pennington, New Jersey. Over the years I became friendly with the husband and wife team of Jim Kinsel and Sherry Dudas who own and operate the organization.

Initially my friendship with Sherry revolved around cooking. We had fun cooking lunch for each other. Both Sherry and her husband were becoming vegetarians.

Although there was no livestock on the farm, there was plenty of wildlife such as deer, birds, raccoons and beaver. Although these animals could be troublesome, Jim and Sherry took great care in handling them. I had great respect for the couple, especially the husband, who never discouraged the animals from their fields by shooting or harming them.

Their farm became so successful it expanded to include two large organic farms. With the ever increasing demands of services and change in personnel, they had hired many new employees. One young man in particular came with good references and credentials, but they were not happy with his performance.

Sherry mentioned that Chip barked whenever he heard the new employee's tractor approaching. Excited that Chip might provide insight into the situation, my friend agreed to a telepathy session.

I decided to first attempt communication with Chip at a distance. Having met Chip several times, I knew what he looked like. He was a mix of lab and perhaps cattle dog, with black with white makings on his front paws. If he was not with either of his people riding in Jim's truck or walking with Sherry, he was tied near his dog house. Having a mental picture of the animal makes it easier for me to make a connection.

I went through the process of grounding or clearing my mind, offering love and then connecting. I started by asking Chip what was happening at the farm. Suddenly a picture came into my mind of a horse plowing a field. The horse was wearing a heavy leather harness with wide leather reins. The horse was working very hard.

I felt disappointed thinking my connection with Chip was not accurate. Later that day I went to the farm to speak to my friend. I told her my distant connection was not good. I described the horse, the harness and reins. Sherry did not share my disappointment.

"That's how Chip feels. I often keep him in this harness when he would rather be free," Sherry explained.

Chip was wearing a harness secured around his face and mussel which is tied to a leash. This style, called a "halty," avoids the use of a choke chain, since the part around his mussel acts as the lead.

What My Dog Told Me About Healthy Eating

    So what I thought was a failed communication seemed to be on track after all. It is not unusual for the communicator to perceive something from the subject that appears irrelevant, but as in my case, these seemingly failed perceptions are really spot on.

    Chip's person, enjoying the natural communication of living in close quarters with her pet, knew exactly how he felt!

Chapter 12

What She Said

> *"19,000 farm animals are killed each minute...when I build my new cow barn we will only be able to keep about a 100 cows ...the real value of a rescue operation is to educate..."*
>
> Mike Stura, Founder of Skylands Animal Sanctuary and Rescue, 2015

Animal communication can be used for fun, enhancing health or closeness during happy or sad times. It takes on a whole different appearance when it is used to communicate with farm animals living in tragic circumstances or marked for an early and painful death.

Farm animal rescue workers can offer great insight into this area of communication, since the nature of their job offers sensitivity to the animals' unfortunate circumstances. Many times they are with the animal during highly emotional and violent times - even before death- and can connect to the animal's feelings.

I had the opportunity to hear a lecture by an impressive volunteer farm animal rescue worker. In his real life he is a truck driver. Mike even bought his own little van to transport his rescues. A large, burly man with long, stringy dark hair and a beard, he did not look like a man I wanted to meet in a dark alley, but he told his story with a soft-spoken gentleness.

"I answered a call to rescue a cow that escaped from a slaughterhouse. The animal had found its way to a parking lot. When I arrived, a slaughterhouse employee was chasing the cow with a rope. The cow lunged and kicked at the employee. The employee threw up his hands in disgust turning the cow over to me." Mike laughed.

"I have to admit I was scared, but I just stood in front of the cow not moving. The cow knew I was not going to hurt him and quietly came up to me."

The volunteer flashed a picture on the screen of himself hugging a cow in a beautiful green pasture-the cow he rescued. The volunteer named him, Mike Jr.

Mike transports many of the animals he rescues to animal sanctuaries. This particular cow he took to Woodstock Farm Animal Sanctuary in Woodstock, New York. "I go to visit him often and he always recognizes me," the volunteer said with great pride.

After the lecture, I approached Mike, thanked him for his presentation and asked his opinion of animal telepathy. His response was, "Whenever I go into a slaughterhouse I sense the overwhelming fear of the animals."

Mike's passion for saving farm animals from harm continues to grow. Since the writing of this little book, Mike and his lovely wife Wendy founded Skylands Animal Sanctuary and Rescue in Wantage, New Jersey.

Farm animal telepathy is a new frontier of animal communication. No doubt it will be challenging since sadness and horror may be the message. However it may result in tremendous insight into the care, breeding, selling and slaughtering of animals. It may even cause some people to stop and think about what they are doing and stop eating meat.

Sometimes I wonder if, all the while I was driving past the grass-fed cattle farm, writing the mad cow article , writing the Singer book review and cooking meatless meals in my kitchen, Mochi was reading my mind and talking to me telepathically so I would finally understand the compassion of my food choices?

You might ask "why would my dog, who is a carnivore, basically tell me not to eat meat and thereby save some cows?"

At different times in her life, Mochi did eat commercial dog food predominately made from lamb, chicken, fish or vegetables. When Mochi was a puppy, at the suggestion of my veterinarian, I tried to feed her dog food made predominantly with beef, but she refused to eat it. Since mad cow was such an issue at this time and in view of her preferences, I decided to avoid feeding her products mainly made with beef.

Also, it is important to remember that she was talking to me about *me,* not telling me her desires for *her.*

Although Mochi never gave me an outward identifiable sign that she was communicating with me about my food choices and treatment of animals, I do remember that during this time she expressed much love and closeness.

Was it Mochi who helped put the thought in my mind the day I drove by the cows and saw them in a different image?

I decided to ask her about it. With Mochi present I asked "Did you help me with my food choices?"

When I posed the question to my dog, the thought that immediately came back was "I always know what you are writing."

At another time, with Mochi at a distance, I asked the question again. A picture came to mind of her smiling, even laughing at me, as if to say "Of course I did!"

What My Dog Told Me About Healthy Eating

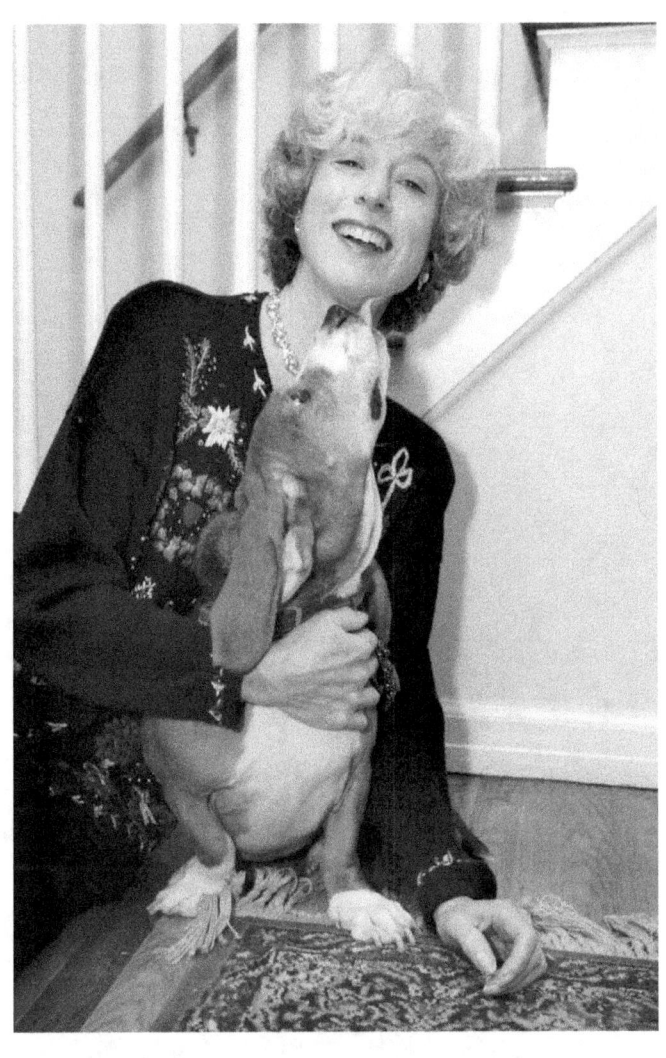

Mochi at age three poses for Christmas Photo.

Credit: Frank Wojciechowski

What My Dog Told Me About Healthy Eating

Acknowledgments

I wish to gratefully thank the special people and animals who made this book possible.

Sally Stang and Diana Rosenberg, my two editors, worked on my book while putting up with my many comments about their suggestions.

Diana Rosenberg also practiced Therapeutic Touch with me.

Frank Wojciechowski, professional photographer, was always generous with his time and patience in his photo shoots of Mochi.

Irma Hardjasumantri, amateur photographer from Indonesia, whose photo of Mochi adorns the cover.

I am forever grateful to Judith Mauro, a special friend of myself and my mother, who encouraged me to finish this book.

Mochi, my strong heart, guided our relationship. I love you forever.

What My Dog Told Me About Healthy Eating

Resources

Animal Communication

J. Allen Boone

Kinship with All Life Harper and Row 1954 and Harper Collins 1976.

Letters to Strongheart Prentice Hall 1939

You are the Adventure! Prentice Hall 1943 and Robert H. Sommer 2007

Patty Summers

Talking with The Animals Harper Roads 1998

Barbara Woodhouse

Talking to Animals Stein and Day 1974

Marta Williams

Learning Their Language: Intuitive Communication with Animals and Nature New World Library 2003

Joe Dwyer

Shelby's Grace from Abused Pub to Angel of Mercy Perennial Press Publishing 2012

Animal Rights

Peter Singer

Animal Liberation, Harper Collins 1975, 1990, 2002

In Defense of Animals Basil Blackwell 1995

Why Our Food Choices Matter with Jim Mason, Rodale 2006

Carol Adams, Patti Breitman, Virginia Messina

Never Too Late To Go Vegan The Experiment 2014

Dudley Giehl

Vegetarianism A Way of Life Harper Row 1979 (out of print but worth obtaining)

Marketing Social Change

Peter Singer

Ethics Into Action, Henry Spira and the Animal Rights Movement

Rowman & Littlefield Publishers Inc. 1998

Nick Cooney

Change of Heart: What Psychology Can Teach Us About Spreading Social Change

Lantern Books 2010

Resources

Therapeutic Touch

Dolores Krieger

The Therapeutic Touch: How to Use Your Hands To Heal Touchstone *1979*

Accepting Your Power to Heal, The Personal Practice of Therapeutic Touch Bear & Company Publishing 1993

Therapeutic Touch Inner Workbook Bear & Company Publishing 1997

Dora van Gelder Kunz

The Personal Aura QuestBooks 1991

Spiritual Healing Quest Books 1995

Caroline Myss

Anatomy of the Spirit, Three River's Press 1996

Diet Approaches to Health

Michio Kushi

The Cancer Prevention Diet St Martin's Press 1993

Dirk Benedict

Confessions of a Kamikaze Cowboy: A True Story of Discovery, Acting, Health, Illness, Recovery, and Life Square One Publishers 2006

Neal Barnard

Reverse Diabetes Now: The Scientifically Proven System for Reversing Diabetes Without Drugs Rodale Inc 2007

Resources

Vegetarian / Vegan Cookbooks

Linda McCartney

Linda's Kitchen: Simple and Inspiring Recipes for Meal-Less Meals Bulfinch 1995

Christina Pirello

Cooking the Whole Foods Way Penguin Group 1997

Jannequin Bennett

The Complete Vegan Kitchen Thomas Nelson 2001

Leslie McEachern

The Angelica Home Kitchen Ten Speed Press 2003

Nava Atlas

Vegan Holiday Kitchen Sterling 2011

What My Dog Told Me About Healthy Eating

Anne and Freya Dinshah

Apples, Bean Dip, & Carrot Cake- Kids Teach Yourself to Cook American Vegan Society 2012

Resources

Online Recipes

Growing up with holiday traditions, I enjoy vegan versions of holiday treats and pass them down to my family and friends. These are two I use frequently. You may want to start your own list.

Irish Soda Bread

http://hellyeahitsvegan.com/vegan-irish-soda-bread/

Hot Cross Buns

http://bitofthegoodstuff.com/2013/03/hot-cross-buns-dairy-free-egg-free-vegan/

Easy Recipes

Vegetarian Chili

Obtained from a friend

Serves 8 but can be easily halved.

Ingredients

1 tablespoon vegetable oil

2 large onions (or 3 medium), diced

2 green peppers, diced

½ to 1 bulb of garlic, crushed or minced

1 26-28 oz. can whole or diced tomatoes

2 tablespoons chili powder (add 3 tablespoons if you want it a bit spicier)

2 teaspoons sea salt

2 teaspoons cumin (powder or seeds)

2 teaspoons oregano

2 teaspoons cocoa

(optional) your favorite hot sauce to taste

1 large (or 3 medium) green or yellow squash, sliced into rings, then quartered

4 large carrots (or 6 medium carrots), sliced

1-2 ears of corn (remove corn from husks)

1 16-19 oz. can red kidney beans, drained

1 16-19 oz. can white kidney beans, drained

1 16-19 oz. can black beans, drained

Sauté chopped onions in vegetable oil until soft, about 4-5 minutes. Add chopped green peppers and garlic. Sauté another 4-5 minutes over medium low heat.

Add tomatoes, chili powder, salt, cumin, oregano, cocoa, and hot sauce. If using whole tomatoes, break them up. Stir all ingredients and bring to a boil. Simmer 5-10 minutes.

Add squash, carrots and corn. Stir well. Cover pot. Simmer 45 minutes over low heat, stirring occasionally. (I usually cook in less time.)

Add beans. Stir well. Simmer another 20 minutes. (I usually cook in less time.)

You can use dried beans too. Just cook them separately until soft.

Serving Suggestions: This chili can be eaten as prepared and also served over hot cooked rice or with vegan corn bread. Chili can be topped with chopped red onion, chives and/or vegan sour cream.

Resources

Basic White Cake

From Christine Pirello's *Cooking the Whole Foods Way.*

I used this recipe hundreds of times for cakes but like it best made into muffins-blueberry! See what kind of a cake or muffin you can make! Great recipe to build on. Get Creative!

The recipe uses brown rice syrup as a sweetener so it is good for diabetics, but if it is not sweet enough for you, add some sugar or preferably maple syrup granules.

Makes 1 cake that serves 6 to 8 people

Ingredients

2 ½ cups whole wheat pastry flour

2 to 3 teaspoons baking powder

1/8 teaspoon sea salt

¼ cup avocado oil (I use canola oil)

½ cup brown rice syrup

1 teaspoon pure vanilla extract

½ cup spring or filtered water

½ to 2/3 cup non-dairy drink such soy or rice milk (I use 1 cup of Amazake Rice Shake instead of water and non-dairy drink to make it smoother.)

Preheat oven to 350F. Lightly oil and flour a 9 inch round cake pan or loaf pan and set aside.

Wisk together flour, baking powder and salt in a bowl. Whisk oil, rice syrup, vanilla, water and ½ cup milk together in another bowl. Stir the liquid mixture into the flour mixture, mixing until smooth; do not overmix. The batter should be thick and spoon able, not runny. Add more milk if needed. Spoon into prepared pan.

Bake on center rack for 40 to 45 minutes, or until a wooden pick inserted in center comes out clean and cake springs back to touch. If you have a hot oven like my 1952 Tappan, you may need to shorten cooking time. Do not open oven door until cake has baked 10-20 minutes or cake may sink.

Cool cake in pan 10 minutes before turning out of pan and cooling on wire rack.

Note: If you substitute gluten free flour for a gluten free cake, you may need to reduce the amount of nondairy drink or water. I find gluten free flour much lighter than whole wheat or white flour.

Pizza Dough

From my mother naturally vegan, except I exchanged brown rice syrup for honey.

1 medium pizza

Serves 2-4 people

Ingredients

1 cup warm water

1 teaspoon brown rice syrup

1 teaspoon oil

¼ teaspoon salt

1 package yeast (1 package equals about 2 teaspoons. I have been having success with Hodgson Mill Active Dry Yeast)

Mix water with yeast and brown rice syrup. Water should be warm not hot. Let stand for 1-2 minutes for yeast action to start.

Stir in flour to make dough.

Knead several minutes to mix ingredients.

Place in stainless steel or oven proof bowel. Cover and leave in a warm place to rise for at least 2 hours.

Prepare and use toppings of your choice.

I sauté Swiss chard or spinach, mushrooms and onions for a few minutes before placing on dough.

Spread dough on oiled pizza pan, preferably stainless steel.

Spread tomato sauce on dough, then top with vegetables ending with non-dairy mozzarella style cheese. Daiya brand melts well.

What My Dog Told Me About Healthy Eating

Avocado Pasta Salad

This cold salad always gets compliments.

1 portion of pasta makes 2-4 servings

Ingredients

1 dry portion of short pasta of your choice. I use casarecce, but penne, rigatoni or gemelli also works well.

1 medium avocado

¼ cup sundried tomatoes

Vegenaise to taste

Prepare the pasta as directed on the product you chose. Suggest sea salt or no salt.

Peel and cut avocado in bite size or slightly larger pieces.

Drain and place pasta in bowel that can be refrigerated.

Add avocado.

Add sun dried tomato.

Let stand 5 to 10 minutes to let pasta cool.

Add Vegenaise to taste.

Refrigerate and serve when ready. Note avocado will darken in several hours so prepare close to time of use.

Animal Sanctuaries

Farm Sanctuary

Animal Protection Organization

3150 Aikens Road, Watkins Glen, NY 14891

www.farmsanctuary.com

Woodstock Farm Sanctuary

Animal Shelter

2 Rescue Road, High Falls, NY 12440

www.woodstocksanctuary.org

Skylands Animal Sanctuary and Rescue

50 Compton Road, Wantage, NJ 07461

www.skylandssanctuary.org

Canine and Feline Advocates

God's Creatures Ministry

P.O. Box 666

Wayne, NJ 07474

www.Godscreaturesministry.org

Joe Dwyer

Motivational Speaker

www.joedwyerspeaking.com

Resources

Grassroots Farm Animal Activists

NJ Farm Animal Save

www.njfarmanimalsave.com

Community Supported Agriculture (CSA)

Honeybrook Organic Farm

260 Wargo Rd, Pennington, NJ 08534

www.honeybrookorganicfarm.com

www.ingramcontent.com/pod-product-compliance
Lightning Source LLC
Chambersburg PA
CBHW072052290426
44110CB00014B/1654